1/07

D1713414

Joseph Lister

Father of Antiseptics

Peggy J. Parks

BLACKBIRCH PRESS

An imprint of Thomson Gale, a part of The Thomson Corporation

Detroit • New York • San Francisco • San Diego • New Haven, Conn.
Waterville, Maine • London • Munich

Photo Credits: Cover: © Bettmann/CORBIS; © Adam Woolfitt/CORBIS, 27; Andrew Lambert Photography/Science Photo Library, 36; © Bettmann/CORBIS, 7, 45; Blackbirch Press, 32; Bridgeman Art Library, 56; Centers for Disease Control and Prevention, 12; CNRI/Photo Researchers, Inc., 16; © CORBIS, 5; Corel Corporation, 10, 19; © Dr. Kessel & Kardon/Tissues & Organs/Visuals Unlimited, 34; © Eric Crichton/CORBIS, 22; George Disario/CORBIS, 41; © Gianni Dagli Orti/CORBIS, 48; © Hulton-Deutsch Collection/CORBIS, 49, 57; Hulton Archive/Getty Images, 20, 43, 50; Image Select/Art Resource, NY, 33; Jim Dowdalls/Photo Researchers, Inc., 24; Neil Borden/Photo Researchers, Inc., 54; Photos.com, 29, 30, 38; Reunion des Musees Nationaux/Art Resource, NY, 17; © Royalty-Free/CORBIS, 14; SPL/Photo Researchers, Inc., 8; Time-Life Pictures/Getty Images, 40

LIBRARY OF CONGRESS CATALOGING-IN-PUBLICATION DATA

Parks, Peggy J., 1951-
  Joseph Lister / by Peggy J. Parks.
    p. cm. — (Giants of science)
  Includes bibliographical references and index.
  ISBN 1-4103-0322-5 (hard cover : alk. paper)
  1. Lister, Joseph, Baron, 1827-1912—Juvenile literature. 2. Surgeons—Great Britain—Biography—Juvenile literature. I. Title. II. Series.

  R489.L75P37 2005   617'.092—dc22

CONTENTS

A Lifesaving Discovery

It was August 12, 1865, and Joseph Lister had dreamed about this day for a long time. He was a surgeon at the Royal Infirmary in Glasgow, Scotland, and had studied infection for years. He had finally developed an antiseptic treatment from carbolic acid, a chemical made from coal tar, and he believed it had the ability to kill germs. If he were right, there was a good chance that deadly infections could be stopped. Yet as confident as he was, Lister knew the only way to test the treatment was on a live patient—but there was a great deal of risk in doing that. There was always the chance that he could harm someone he was trying to help. He knew, though, that he had to take the risk. People were dying of infection, and he was determined to do something about it.

Eleven-year-old Jimmy Greenlees had been brought to the infirmary after being run over by a horse-drawn cart. The boy's leg was broken in several places and had a gaping wound where the bone protruded through his skin. This injury, known as a compound fracture, was life threatening. In those days, serious wounds such as compound fractures almost always developed deadly sepsis, or infection. Lister knew that most surgeons would amputate the injured limb right away, before infection set in, even though amputations often led to death as well. Lister did not want such a young boy to lose a leg, so he decided instead to treat the boy's wounds with antiseptics.

Lister carefully cleaned the wound with a carbolic acid solution. Then he dressed the wound with carbolic acid, which he

---

British surgeon Joseph Lister is renowned for developing the first antiseptic treatment to kill the germs responsible for infections.

had mixed with putty to hold the dressing in place. The putty would also form a seal to keep germs out. The last step was to splint the boy's leg and then apply a bandage to hold the carbolic acid putty and splint in place.

Over the next several days, Lister kept the bandage wet with carbolic acid. On the fourth day, the time when infections usually set in, he removed the bandage and looked underneath—and he was overjoyed. His treatment had worked! The wound had no pus, no swelling, no odor, and no sign of infection whatsoever. By using his unusual germ-killing remedy, Lister had saved not only the boy's leg, but also his life. The young patient fully recovered.

A Quiet Hero

Lister lived in the nineteenth century, a time when medicine was crude and infection was not understood. Most doctors of that era accepted infection as an unfortunate but inevitable result of serious injuries. Although they did not know what caused infection, most assumed it was the result of oxygen or some other type of gas in the air. Lister proved that idea to be wrong—infection was the direct result of germs.

"He taught . . . that there was a right way and a wrong way of doing everything . . . and that the least complaint of pain or uneasiness demanded immediate attention."
—ARCHIBALD MALLOCK, SURGEON, REFERRING TO JOSEPH LISTER

After his successful treatment of Jimmy Greenlees, Lister continued experimenting with carbolic acid on different types of injuries and wounds. The results were dramatic—the rate of infection and death in his surgical wards sharply declined. By 1880 the treatment known as Listerism was being adopted in hospitals throughout the world. Cases of infection were decreasing rapidly and large numbers of patients' lives were being saved.

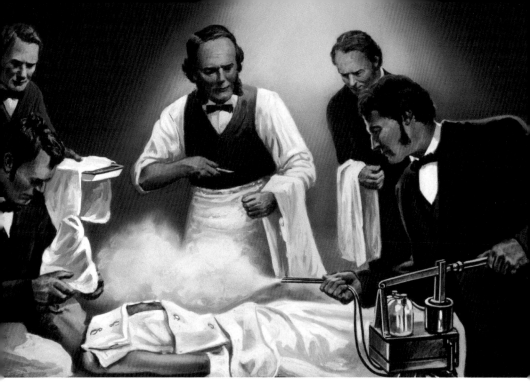

In this painting, Joseph Lister (center) directs his assistant to spray carbolic acid over a patient during one of the first antiseptic surgeries.

Unlike many doctors of his time, Lister was not proud or arrogant, nor did he seek fame or fortune. He was a quiet hero who cared deeply for his patients and wanted to save their lives. His legacy was making surgery safe. Because of his work, his research, and his deep convictions, hospitals became sterile environments where people were often cured, rather than places where they almost always went to die. The story of Joseph Lister—the surgeon who became known as the "father of antiseptic surgery"—began in England, where he was born and raised.

The Quaker Family

Joseph Lister was born on April 5, 1827, at a large mansion in an English country village called Upton. He was the fourth child of Joseph Jackson Lister, a wealthy wine merchant and amateur scientist, and Isabella Harris Lister, a former reading and writing teacher. The Listers were Quakers, followers of a religion that was also known as the Society of Friends. They had plenty of

Lister's father, Joseph Jackson Lister, is pictured here with his most notable invention, the achromatic microscope.

money, but they were humble people. In accordance with their faith, they believed that no man or woman was better than any other, no matter how blessed he or she was with worldly goods. Like all Quakers, they dressed in plain gray or black clothing and gave generously to people who were in need.

Although their religion forbade the Listers to dance or play music in their home, their household was a lively place where the family had fun and enjoyed being together. Upton House, as the Lister home was known, was a sprawling estate on nearly seventy acres of land. Along with his brothers and sisters, Joseph spent a great deal of time exploring and playing outside. He was always fascinated with nature and loved being outdoors.

In addition to being devoted to their religious faith, the Listers were passionate about knowledge, especially science. This was mostly due to the influence of Joseph Jackson Lister, who had been interested in science for most of his life. His formal schooling had ended by the time he was fourteen years old, when he quit school to enter his father's wine-importing business. Yet even though he no longer attended classes, he taught himself science and mathematics. Along with a close friend, Lister studied the characteristics of blood, and together they published their findings. But his most notable achievement was even more important to the scientific world—perfecting the microscope by inventing a type of lens known as the achromatic lens. Before Lister's invention, scientists did not find microscopes to be very useful. The devices were mounted with only a single lens, which provided a distorted view of the material being examined. As a result, even the most astute scientists avoided using the instrument altogether. Lister's achromatic lens changed that forever. The achromatic lens was made of several different types of glass that were placed at precise distances from each other. The compound system eliminated the vision flaws and caused a great demand for microscopes. It also led to Lister's election into England's Royal Society, an esteemed organization through which the British government supported science.

Early Schooling in England

From the time Joseph was a small boy, he shared his father's love of science. He was also fascinated with medicine, and at a very young age he announced to his family that he would someday become a surgeon. This was surprising to them because no one in the family, with the exception of a distant cousin, had ever embarked on a medical career of any sort. Joseph's father was mildly disapproving of his son's career choice because he believed nature should be left alone to heal people. Lister could see how determined young Joseph was to become a surgeon, however, so he did not try to discourage him.

"Either the thing should be done properly or not at all."
—JOSEPH LISTER

Joseph received his early schooling at home, tutored by his mother and father. Historians believe this was likely because he had a speech impediment, as biographer Richard B. Fisher explains: "To a sensitive boy, the affliction must have been a serious embarrassment. Throughout his life it tended to appear when he became tense or excited. . . . [He] was always conscious of the stammer and was said in later life to have referred to it as a severe thorn in the flesh.'"[1]

When Joseph was eleven years old, his parents decided that he was ready for a formal education, and he was sent to the Hitchin School, a private school for Quaker children. He excelled in all his classes, but by far his favorite subjects were those related to science. His schoolmaster, Isaac Brown, reported to Joseph's parents that their son was progressing very well and that his conduct was favorable. However, Brown must have caught the boy misbehaving from time to time, because he wrote that Joseph was "full of spirits, which sometimes cause him to overstep the rules of order and bring him a little into disgrace."[2]

As a young man, Joseph Lister frequently dissected frogs in order to learn more about their anatomy.

In 1840, when Joseph was thirteen, his father transferred him to a more advanced Quaker school known as Grove House. Joseph was happy there and was placed among the school's top students. During his years at Grove House, Joseph's interest in science and medicine continued to grow. He worked in the school's science laboratory, where he was responsible for washing the lab equipment and other tasks. When he had free time or was on holidays away from school, he often carried out scientific experiments. He once dissected a sheep's head, and he also frequently dissected fish, frogs, and other small creatures. When he was finished dissecting, he made elaborate drawings of the skeletons.

Difficult Times

In the spring of 1844, soon after Joseph turned seventeen, he left Grove House and moved to London, where he attended University College. Lister encouraged his son to study a wide variety of subjects in addition to science. He assured Joseph that a well-rounded education would be valuable in life, as well as in a medical career. Joseph heeded his father's advice and enrolled in a bachelor of arts program. His studies included Greek, Latin, and philosophy, as well as mathematics, anatomy, and other sciences. For an essay he wrote about chemistry, he was awarded a prestigious silver medal.

Yet even though college was going well for Joseph, his second year was a difficult and painful time. His oldest brother, John, developed a brain tumor and died in October 1846 at the age of twenty-four. Joseph was brokenhearted over the loss, and he became depressed. Despite his difficulties, though, he managed to continue his studies. In December 1847 he graduated with a bachelor of arts degree and enrolled in University College's medical school.

Joseph had looked forward to his medical training, but he found his first year to be a great disappointment. He had moved into a boardinghouse run by an elderly and strict Quaker man, and the household was gloomy compared to his own lively family home. He was also lonely. Although he got

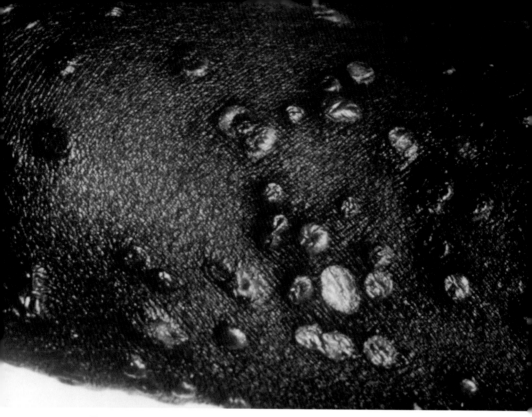

This is a close-up view of skin covered with smallpox, which Lister suffered from as a young man.

along well with his fellow students, he was too introverted and shy to make any close friends. In addition, he was still mourning his brother's death, and as time passed he became increasingly depressed.

Joseph's problems grew worse when he was stricken with a case of smallpox. His illness was not severe, but it left him physically weak. He did not give himself ample time to recover. He returned to classes and worked relentlessly at his studies, taking little or no time to rest. As a result, in early 1848 he collapsed and his doctors declared that he had suffered a nervous breakdown.

Afterwards, Joseph found himself too depressed to do much of anything, including work. He lost the enthusiasm and motivation for which he had been known throughout his life. He even began to question whether he would ever be qualified to practice surgery as well as whether he should become a surgeon at all. Concerned about his physical and mental health, Joseph's family appealed to him to drop out of school for a while and take a long holiday. He heeded their advice and left the country to spend some time traveling in Ireland.

Return to Medical School

The months Lister spent away from England helped him recover and regain his strength. In the winter of 1848 he returned to London and reenrolled at the University College medical school. Besides being physically and mentally stronger, he also had a renewed sense of purpose and was more determined than ever to succeed. He did well in his classes and won various honors and medals for his superior work. His professors considered him a brilliant student with a secure future as a surgeon.

> "He was full of sympathy for suffering, and would devote himself to the relief of a patient without consideration of time or trouble."
> —WATSON CHEYNE, A SURGEON AND LISTER'S LONGTIME ASSISTANT

In the fall of 1850 Lister began his medical residency at University College Hospital. This allowed him to move out of the boardinghouse and into the hospital living quarters with other medical students. The atmosphere was cheerful, and Lister was much happier there than he had been at the gloomy Quaker home. During this time he also joined the debating and medical societies, where he was warmly welcomed by the other members. Through his involvement in these organizations, he managed to overcome his shyness and make new friends.

During his residency, Lister continued to study science and medicine. He frequently attended lectures in clinical surgery that were given by John Eric Erichsen, who was professor of surgery. In early 1851 he accepted a position as Erichsen's dresser,

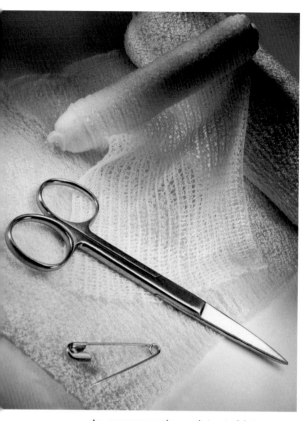

As a surgeon's assistant, Lister routinely dressed wounds. He was appalled by the high rate of infection among his patients.

the name for a surgeon's assistant. Dressers were selected from the school's best students, and their training period lasted about three months. Lister reported to Henry Thompson, the house surgeon, who was second in command after Erichsen. His duties included taking patient case histories, writing case notes, and assisting Thompson as necessary.

Houses of Death

As highly regarded as Lister was, he had a quality that his supervisors —and even his own father—saw as a major flaw for a surgeon: He was extremely sensitive. It deeply disturbed him that patients were so often plagued by infection, and especially that so many of them died once they were in the hospital. He was bothered by a common phrase among the medical staff: "The operation was a success, but the patient died." Unlike experienced surgeons, who seemed hardened to the misery within the hospital walls, Lister took the suffering personally. He refused to accept that such anguish should be common or expected, and he was constantly troubled by it.

Lister also found the conditions in the hospital deplorable. There was little or no regard for cleanliness, which was thought to be frivolous and unnecessary. In an effort to save the cost of soap, patients were not given baths and surgeons rarely washed their hands—even between one operation and the next. They wore the same coats for months without laundering them, because dirty, stained surgical coats were considered a sign of a surgeon's popularity. Operating rooms were filthy, and there was no procedure for sterilizing surgical instruments. Perhaps the worst thing of all was that surgeons were not judged by how skilled they were, but rather by how fast they could perform operations. Yet in spite of these conditions and the constant suffering Lister saw around him, he would not turn away from his chosen profession. Instead, he vowed to work toward changing things for the better.

One form of infection that Lister observed was gangrene. This was one of the most deadly infections of all because it made body tissue literally rot away. Once patients developed gangrene, their chances of survival were extremely slim. Because gangrene and other infections were so common in surgical wards, they were referred to as hospital diseases, or simply hospitalism. In fact, people typically thought of hospitals as places where people were almost certain to die, as biographer Rhoda Truax explains: "No one knew just why a hospital should be a house of death, but there were plenty of explanations, the most popular of which was that miasmas [poisonous air] or gases hovered about hospitals, entering the wounds and causing them to rot. Where these miasmas came from nobody could say. It was easy to lay the blame on something vague and general."[3]

An even more common belief about hospital diseases was that they were caused by oxygen in the air. However, there was a major flaw with this theory that no one could explain: The same amount of oxygen was everywhere, including in people's homes. Yet patients who were treated in their homes—even those who underwent amputations—had a much lower rate of infection and death than people who were treated in hospitals. This fact was so disturbing that some doctors believed all hospitals should be demolished.

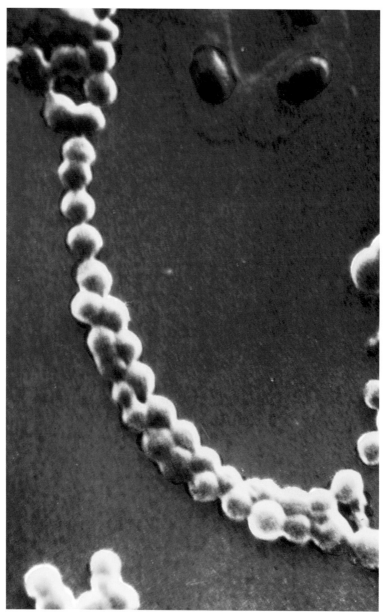

This is a highly magnified image of the bacteria that cause gangrene, a deadly infection that causes body tissue to rot.

Studying Infection

Lister was not convinced that any of the common theories about infection were correct. As a dresser, he had assisted when Erichsen treated wounds by cauterizing (burning) them with chemicals. Lister observed that even though most patients with gangrene died, some managed to survive after their wounds were cauterized. He found this puzzling, and he began to think that something in the wound had caused the infection, rather than oxygen or anything hovering in the air. He reasoned that once this "something" had been burned away, the infection had disappeared and the patient's wounds were able to heal.

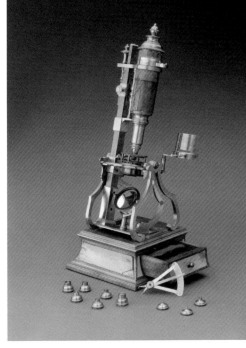

Lister examined samples of gangrenous tissue under a microscope in order to determine the cause of the infection.

In June 1851 Lister was assigned to a temporary position as house surgeon. As he spent greater amounts of time in the surgical wards, he became even more determined to understand the real cause of infection. His father had given him a fine microscope, and Lister began to spend all his free time experimenting with it. He took samples of infected tissue from patients suffering with gangrene, and night after night he examined the tissue. In the process, he observed a microscopic species that he had never seen before. He wondered if it could be some type of fungus that grew inside diseased tissue, much like fungus that grew on trees. It was a concept he had never heard of and he found it intriguing. He drew sketches of what he had observed, and he also wrote two papers entitled "Gangrene" and "Use of the Microscope in Medicine." Even though the microscope was not yet considered very valuable by medical professionals, Lister knew it was a powerful diagnostic tool. He was determined to use it for further research into infection.

Lister the Surgeon

In addition to examining infected tissue, Lister used his microscope for other types of experiments. For instance, he was interested in studying the tissue of microscopic muscles, such as those in the iris of the eye. He wanted to better understand how the iris dilated and contracted, which regulated the size of the pupil. He also studied muscles of the skin because he was fascinated with how they erected tiny hair shafts that formed goose bumps. He did not pursue these experiments in great depth, but his research was considered significant. He later wrote a paper about his findings entitled "Observations on the Muscular Tissue of the Skin," which included his original illustrations. That paper, as well as one he had written about the muscular tissues of the eye, was later printed in a leading scientific publication, the *Quarterly Journal of Microscopical Science.*

Lister's term as house surgeon came to an end in February 1852. He had completed all the required formal training and was eligible to take his examinations. However, he believed he would benefit from gaining additional medical experience, so he accepted a position as clinical clerk to the senior house physician, Walter H. Walshe.

Later that year, Lister took examinations in anatomy, physiology, pathology, and surgery, and he performed exceptionally well on all of them. In December 1852 he graduated from University College with honors, earning a bachelor of medicine degree. In addition, he was awarded the distinction of Fellow of the Royal College of Surgeons. Lister was now a highly trained medical professional who was fully qualified to practice surgery.

Trip to Scotland

With his formal training behind him, Lister was not in a hurry to set up a surgical practice of his own. His family was financially secure and his father was willing to continue supporting him, so he had no immediate need to start earning a salary. Also, he believed there was much to gain by continuing to work with experienced physicians. So, in February 1853, he became a physician's assistant to Walshe. The position was the equivalent of being a house surgeon, and it lasted for five months.

When his term with Walshe was over, Lister began to ponder his future career plans. During medical school he had grown to admire and respect a physiology professor named William Sharpey, so he decided to ask Sharpey for advice. The professor suggested that Lister travel to Edinburgh, Scotland, and spend about a month there. Edinburgh was the home of Sharpey's closest friend, James Syme, who was the professor of clinical surgery at Edinburgh University and a noted surgeon at the Royal Infirmary. Sharpey believed Lister would benefit from attending Syme's clinical lectures as well as observing how he conducted himself with patients in his surgical wards.

Lister decided to follow his professor's recommendation, and in September 1853 he traveled to Scotland. He moved his belongings into a house in Edinburgh, and then went to visit Syme. Along with him, he carried a letter of recommendation from Sharpey.

In 1853 Lister went to Edinburgh, Scotland, to study under surgeon James Syme, a university professor of clinical surgery.

This portrait shows the young Lister in 1855, the year he became assistant surgeon at the Royal Infirmary.

Friend and Mentor

Soon after Lister met Syme for the first time, he knew the two were destined to become close friends. He took an immediate liking to the surgeon, and could see that Syme was highly respected and admired by the medical students and Royal Infirmary staff. Observing Syme during surgical procedures and listening to him lecture, Lister found him tremendously inspiring. He admired the professor so much, in fact, that instead of staying in Edinburgh for a month, as he had planned, he decided to remain there longer. Syme was delighted with Lister's decision to stay on, and appointed him as his supernumerary clerk, a position that involved duties similar to those of a house surgeon.

The longer Lister worked with Syme, the more he grew to admire him. Over time, he even began thinking of the professor as a second father, and Syme felt equally close to his young protégé. When Syme's house surgeon was called away in January 1854, he offered the position to Lister, who gladly accepted.

A Budding Relationship

As Syme and Lister became closer, the young surgeon was a frequent visitor to Syme's home, a country estate known as Millbank. Lister felt comfortable there because it reminded him of his own family's home in England. Another reason

Lister enjoyed being at Millbank was his growing friendship with Syme's eldest daughter, Agnes. She was attractive and fun to be with, as well as highly intelligent. It was obvious to Lister that Agnes had been raised by a surgeon, as she was perfectly comfortable talking about medical and scientific issues—a highly unusual trait in young women of her day. Lister treasured the time they spent together, especially their long, meaningful conversations.

Yet as much as Lister had grown to love the Syme family and his work at the Royal Infirmary, his term as house surgeon was coming to an end. He would no longer have a formal position in Edinburgh, so he contemplated traveling throughout Europe and then returning to London, where he would set up his own practice. He was reluctant to do so for several reasons, however, the most important of which was his affection for Agnes Syme. So when he learned that one of Syme's staff surgeons had died, he quickly applied for the vacant post. In April 1855 Lister was elected a Fellow of the Royal College of Surgeons of Edinburgh and appointed assistant surgeon at the Royal Infirmary.

Soon after that, Lister traveled to Paris to observe surgical practices in clinics. He spent at least three hours each day perfecting his surgical techniques by working on cadavers, dead bodies used for research. He was busy, but he was also homesick, because Agnes was constantly on his mind. After a month in Paris, he returned to Edinburgh and asked Syme for his daughter's hand in marriage. With Syme's blessing, Lister asked Agnes to marry him and she accepted.

"If Professor Lister's conclusions with regard to the power of carbolic acid in compound fractures should be confirmed . . . it will be difficult to overrate the importance of what we may really call his discovery."
—JAMES SYME

Only one thing marred the happiness Lister felt over his impending marriage to Agnes: her religion. She was a member of the Episcopal Church of Scotland, and she had no intention of changing her religion or leaving her church. The only way Lister could marry her was if he renounced his Quaker faith. Although the decision was difficult for him and his family, he chose to join the Symes' church. On April 23, 1856, he and Agnes were married in the drawing room at Millbank. Following the wedding, the newlyweds left for a four-month trip through Europe.

Working Honeymoon

The Listers' first stop was in England, where they spent four weeks. They traveled to Upton House so Agnes could meet her new husband's family, and from there they crossed the English Channel to Brussels, Belgium. Their journey took them to Switzerland, Italy, Germany, Czechoslovakia, Austria, and France—but their honeymoon was far from just a sight-seeing adventure. In almost every city to which they traveled, they visited leading medical schools, hospitals, medical museums, and laboratories. They spent time meeting with doctors, surgeons, and university professors to discuss all things related to medicine.

In 1856 the newly married Lister took his bride Agnes for a visit to Upton House, his family home in Oxfordshire, England.

In October 1856 the Listers returned home to Edinburgh and moved into their new home. It was just a fifteen-minute walk from the Royal Infirmary, where Lister would begin his new position as Syme's assistant surgeon.

Research Partners

Along with Lister's new job came increased responsibilities, so his schedule was extremely hectic. As Syme's assistant, he could be called to the hospital for urgent matters at any time during the day and night. He was often in complete charge of the surgical wards, which involved making rounds with medical students as well as performing surgery on patients. There were also teaching obligations, including the preparation of lectures. Despite his professional obligations, though, Lister still spent as much time as possible doing research. Agnes became his loyal assistant, and together they turned a back kitchen of their home into a laboratory. As Lister performed his various experiments, Agnes neatly and meticulously recorded his findings in research journals.

Laboratory Experiments

With Agnes at his side, Lister used his microscope to study problems that had long intrigued him. An issue of particular interest dealt with the coagulation of blood, which at the time was considered one of the great mysteries of science. Why did blood remain in a fluid state in the arteries and veins only as long as the vessel was intact? What caused it to clot as soon as there was damage to the vessel, or whenever blood came into contact with anything but the vessel's own inner coating? And when a patient was bleeding, what caused the blood to clot on the surface of a wound? After closely studying the circulatory system of frogs, Lister learned that clotting was directly related to the condition of the blood vessels. If they were damaged or irritated in some way, blood would coagulate inside them. Blood would also clot as a protective measure. If there was a cut in the skin, blood clotted over the cut to prevent foreign particles from entering the bloodstream.

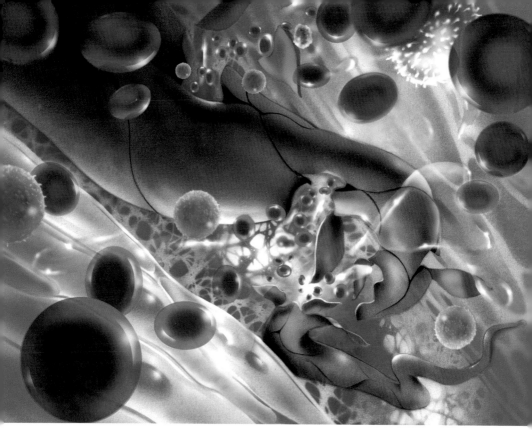

In his research, Lister learned that damaged blood vessels, like this one in a computerized illustration, cause the blood to coagulate.

In addition to blood properties, Lister extensively studied inflammation. Time after time in his surgical wards, he had observed that inflammation (which showed up as swelling or redness) was a sure sign that infection had set in. If he could learn what caused inflammation, perhaps he could also unlock the secrets of infection.

Lister often used live frogs and bats for his experiments. First, he used a chemical such as chloroform to anesthetize the creatures so they would not feel pain. Then he used different methods of irritating their arteries so he could study the effects of the irritation. For instance, he put a drop of extremely cold water on the foot of a frog, and then kept increasing the temperature of the water to study what happened to the blood when it was heated. He observed that as he continued to apply greater amounts of heat, the blood flow slowed down, and then the blood clotted into a mass. He also studied bats and frogs by rubbing various substances into their skin, including a strong solution of salt, caustic ammonia, iodine, turpentine, and several types of acid.

Lister was enthused about his findings. He could see that there was a direct relationship between tissues (such as the frog's skin) and the nervous system. When tissues were irritated, this interfered with their ability to carry out their normal functions and they became inflamed. Lister concluded that the same thing happened in humans. This did not provide all the answers he sought about infection, but he believed he was definitely headed in the right direction.

"To his students, it seemed puzzling that a surgeon would interest himself in such things as test tubes and microscopes."
—SHERWIN B. NULAND, WRITING OF LISTER IN HIS BOOK, *DOCTORS: THE BIOGRAPHY OF MEDICINE*

A New Opportunity

Following his experiments, Lister wrote three scientific papers: "An Inquiry Regarding the Parts of the Nervous System Which Regulate the Contractions of the Arteries," "On the Cutaneous Pigmentary System of the Frog," and the longest and most involved paper, "On the Early Stages of Inflammation." All three papers were published in an 1858 Royal Society journal called *Philosophical Transactions*. He was proud of his experiments, and he believed the papers represented some of his most important work. Years later, he remarked: "If my works are read when I am gone, these will be the ones most highly thought of."[4]

Lister's reputation as a researcher and teacher began to spread. In 1858 Syme was contacted by the University of

Glasgow. The professor of surgery had retired and Syme was asked to speak to his son-in-law about the opportunity. After their discussion, Lister applied for the position and was hired. In the spring of 1860 the Listers moved to Glasgow, a city that was twice the size of Edinburgh.

Life in Glasgow

Lister and his wife settled into their new home in early May and he began teaching at the university. It was summer term and his schedule was not as busy as usual. He gave lectures in pathology and surgery, although his audience was rather small because few students attended school during the summer months.

For the first time in his career, Lister's professional responsibilities were limited to teaching, because he did not have hospital privileges. He had applied for a position at the Royal Infirmary soon after he arrived in Glasgow, but his application was rejected. This annoyed him, as he had fully expected to work as a surgeon as well as a professor. The fact that he could not do so was no reflection on his abilities, but was rather the result of a weak relationship between the hospital and the university.

Although Lister could not practice surgery at the hospital, he did maintain a small private practice of his own. Still, even with his teaching duties, his schedule was not as hectic as it had been in Edinburgh, and this left him more time for research. He and Agnes again set up a home laboratory, and he continued his studies in blood clotting and inflammation. He also wrote and published a number of scientific papers.

Lister also spent time creating a new invention: a type of specialized surgical needle. Most surgeons of that era used a common needle and silk thread to make sutures (or stitches) during an operation. Lister had heard about a new type of suture made from silver wire, which provided a tighter and sturdier incision than silk. The challenge was that even thin wire would not fit through the eye of an average needle. So, he devised a wire needle that would accommodate the metal thread. Lister's invention was widely used after that, but few people knew it was his creation because he never claimed credit for it. As was typical of him, he was not interested in recognition or personal gain. His only motive was to improve surgical techniques for the benefit of patients.

Favorite Professor

In the fall of 1860 Lister gave an introductory speech at the university, and the lecture hall was filled with people. From the very first, his students responded favorably to their professor's intelligence and his warm personality. He spoke of the importance of surgery, but he also showed that he was a humble man by quoting a favorite phrase by French surgeon Ambroise Paré: "I dressed him, God cured him."[5]

Lister soon became immensely popular with the students. They were completely devoted to him and attended his lectures with enthusiasm, often breaking into applause afterward. To show their loyalty and support, they made him honorary president of their medical society. They also prepared a document

In 1860 Lister moved to Glasgow to assume his new position as professor of surgery at the University of Glasgow, shown here.

endorsing Lister's appointment as surgeon to the Glasgow Royal Infirmary, and 161 students signed it.

Although months passed before a final decision was made, Lister was finally elected to the position in August 1861. He was now officially a senior surgeon at the hospital, as well as a respected university professor.

Harsh Realities

Lister was glad to be back in the hospital. Although he enjoyed teaching, he had missed working with patients. But after being away for a year, he had lost touch with the realities of a surgical ward. Once again, he was sickened by the amount of pain and suffering he witnessed. Another factor that disturbed him was the conditions in the Royal Infirmary. Even though the hospital was relatively new and modern, it was a bleak, depressing place. Glasgow was an industrial city filled with factories and shipyards, and many workers suffered serious injuries while on the job. Large numbers of them were admitted to the hospital, which was frequently overcrowded, often with more than one patient in a bed. As Lister had witnessed in previous hospitals, there was dirt and filth everywhere. Virtually every surgical incision became infected, and cases of gangrene were rampant.

Lister was tormented over the widespread infection, and again he searched for answers. Because of the unclean and unsanitary surroundings, he began to wonder if the culprit was dirt. As was true in other hospitals, keeping costs down was a far greater priority than cleanliness. When patients were put in beds, they lay on the same dirty bed linens that previous patients had used. The floors were caked with dirt, vomit, and blood, and doctors and nurses did not wash their hands. Lister was disgusted, and he recalled his studies of inflammation. Through his microscope, he had observed that dirt and bits of foreign matter seemed to cause irritation to a frog's tissue, but he had not thought much about it at the time. For years he had been convinced that an unidentified phenomenon caused infection, and that it was not caused by anything in the air. Could the cause of infection possibly be dirt?

Lister had no idea if this was true, but he was convinced that cleanliness was essential in the hospital. Disregarding the directive of the Royal Infirmary management, he vowed to improve the conditions of his surgical wards. He directed the housekeeping staff to scrub the floors with hot water and soap, and to keep fresh, clean linens on the beds. Bandages were to be clean and sterilized, and staff members were ordered to frequently wash their hands. Even if cleanliness could not prevent infection, Lister believed it would create a much better environment for healing. It would also help patients be more comfortable.

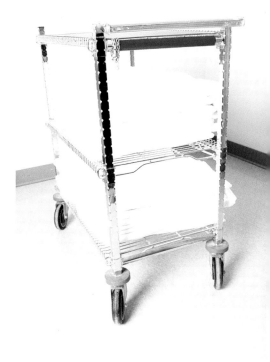

The Mystery of Infection

Over the next few years, Lister grew to be highly respected by his students and by his peers at the Royal Infirmary. He was a skilled surgeon who had proven that he

To help sanitize the Royal Infirmary, Lister ordered clean linens to be kept on hospital beds.

could perform difficult operations with ease. He also developed new techniques for surgery, one of which was excision. Lister used this on patients who suffered from an affliction called tuberculosis of the joint. It was a serious disease, and surgeons almost always treated it by amputating the infected limb. Lister despised amputation, and believed the only time it should be used was when there was no other way to save a patient's life. His excision technique involved removing only the portion of bone or joints that were diseased. As a result, patients were cured without having to lose a hand, an arm, or a leg.

As the number of deaths from infection in his wards decreased, Lister insisted that all surgical tools be regularly sterilized.

As time went by, Lister continued to insist that his surgical wards be kept spotless, and not overly crowded. This caused a strain between him and the hospital directors, who believed his practices were costing them too much money. Nearly all of his demands were met, however. The name of Joseph Lister was becoming well known, and the hospital knew he was an asset to their staff. Moreover, even though no one was exactly certain why, the death rate in his wards was lower than in other areas in the hospital. Some people attributed this to cleanliness, while others believed it was because he and his staff did a better job of monitoring their patients. A few insisted it was just good luck.

In spite of his progress, Lister still believed infection happened far too frequently. His studies of inflammation had caused him to draw several conclusions. One was that putrefaction (the decomposition or rotting of tissue) led to suppuration. This was the formation of pus, which was a sign of infection. He believed the putrefaction was somehow related to the air, although he knew the air alone was not causing it. He was certain that an unidentified foreign substance was entering wounds, which somehow led to infection. Dr. Sherwin B. Nuland explains: "Lister imagined it to fall in from the air in which it lived. All that remained was to identify that invisible *thing*, and then to figure out a way to destroy it."[6]

The Revelation

Thomas Anderson, a chemistry professor at the University of Glasgow, knew of Lister's interest in the study of infection. He also knew Lister did not read scientific literature very often, but he wanted to make him aware of some papers written by Louis Pasteur, a well-known French chemist. Pasteur had published the results of his extensive research on fermentation. Anderson was quite sure the papers would be of interest to Lister, so in early 1865 he visited the surgeon to tell him about Pasteur's work.

Pasteur had studied what he called "the world of the infinitely small," which was how he referred to bacteria. His experiments involved the study of milk and alcohol. Peering through a microscope, he observed thousands of microorganisms and saw that they reproduced at a rapid rate. He became convinced that microbes (microscopic germs) were responsible for the fermentation of the liquids. He also concluded that microbes caused the liquids to sour, or putrefy, and that they had entered the liquids from the outside —which meant these germs were living in the air.

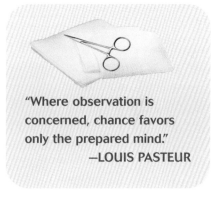

"Where observation is concerned, chance favors only the prepared mind."
—LOUIS PASTEUR

The notion of germs in the air was unheard of. Many scientists believed they were formed through spontaneous generation, meaning they appeared out of nowhere. Pasteur scoffed at this notion. Germs were living things, and he was convinced they could only be reproduced only from germs that already existed. His theory was that they were carried on microscopic particles of dust floating in the atmosphere, and that the particles were more abundant in some places than in others. In addition, he found that germs did not live only in the air. Once they had been transferred to other substances, including solids or liquids, they could exist almost anywhere—and no matter where they lived, they had the ability to reproduce at an astounding rate. He also found that some types of bacteria could only grow when no oxygen was present. This was known as anaerobic bacteria.

Lister read the articles Pasteur had written over and over again, and he was stunned. Even though Pasteur had not connected putrefaction with infected wounds, Lister did so immediately. Suddenly it was all so clear: Putrefaction occurred because of bacteria that lived and thrived in the air as well as in other substances. Of course, Lister reasoned, that meant bacteria could also live and thrive in damaged human flesh. Once germs found their way into wounds, they began to grow and multiply at a rapid rate, and the result was infection.

Lister recalled his studies of inflammation, when he had seen something under his microscope that he thought was a type of fungus. Now he realized he had been looking at germs, although he had not known what they were. These microscopic bacteria fell onto injured tissues and caused them to putrefy, as Truax explains:

Louis Pasteur conducts experiments in his laboratory. Building on Pasteur's work, Lister connected putrefaction with infection.

Microbes swarmed in the air, doing no damage until they gained access to material upon which they could feed. Then they got to work—useful work in some cases, he realized, for the great picture of life could scarcely be painted without including decay. But decay had no place on the bodies of the living, where it caused the horrible septic diseases that made surgical wards places for men to shun. Little microscopic creatures were to blame, creatures which lived and multiplied and which could be killed or rendered powerless if one knew how. It was as simple as that![7]

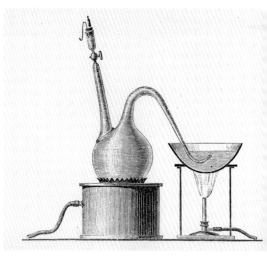

This experiment conducted by Louis Pasteur proved that airborne germs were responsible for fermentation and putrefaction.

Close Study of Bacteria

This discovery about bacteria clarified something that had puzzled and disturbed Lister for many years. He now knew the reason gangrene spread so fast within surgical wards. Millions of germs from just one gangrenous wound could collect in the air, on surgeons' hands, on surgical instruments, on towels and bedding—everywhere. And once they did, they could quickly find their way into other patients' wounds. Suddenly Lister knew why patients who underwent amputations in their homes survived more often than those in the hospital—hospitals were veritable breeding grounds for germs.

Lister had no doubt that his theory was correct, but he also knew that he needed to prove it. Pasteur and other scientists had found that germs bred certain types of disease, but no one had ever connected germs with infection. Lister decided

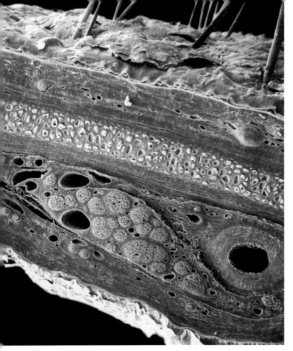

A cross-section shows the layers of human skin, which prevent bacteria from entering the body's interior.

it was up to him to make that connection. He had to prove that bacteria caused infection, and the only way he could do that was to perform extensive research on his own.

With Agnes assisting, Lister repeated all of Pasteur's experiments in his own laboratory. First he used his microscope to study different types of soured liquids, as well as samples of infected blood. He could see that germs were alive and swarming in them all. His next task was to prove that germs could make their way into liquids, and then grow rapidly. He filled four glass flasks with a sugar-water mixture. One had a short, straight neck that was directly exposed to the air, while the other three had necks that were bent at sharp angles. Lister boiled the liquid in the flasks in order to kill any germs that were already present, and then left the containers alone. Several days later he examined the liquid that was exposed to the air, and he found that it was filled with bacteria. The liquid in the other three flasks was clear because germs had been unable to find their way in.

Lister knew this explained the relationship between germs and infection. Human skin, he reasoned, performed much like the glass of a beaker. It was delicate, but provided a covering that protected vulnerable tissue from germs. When a wound caused a break in the skin, there was nothing to stop bacteria from getting in. But as positive as he was about this theory, he still faced the challenge of convincing others—and he had learned through the years how difficult that could be. Surgeons and other medical professionals were not often open to ideas that radically differed from what they had long believed.

Discovery of Antiseptics

Lister, like Pasteur before him, had used heat in his experiments because high temperatures destroyed microbes. Obviously, he could not boil a human wound the way he had boiled liquid. Nor could he apply high heat to a wound because it would be too painful for the patient. Wounds could be stitched more tightly, but that would only keep new bacteria out; it would not do anything to destroy germs that were already living inside a wound. What Lister needed was a way to destroy the germs—and destroy them quickly—in the wound itself, as he explained: "If the wound could be treated with some substance which, without doing serious mischief to the human tissues, would kill the microbes already contained in it, and prevent the further access of others in the living state, putrefaction might be prevented however freely the air with its oxygen should enter."[8]

Lister spent hours poring over documents, scientific papers, and medical journals in search of an answer. He had read about antiseptics, which were sometimes used to purify hospital rooms when the odor of gangrene became overpowering. He believed that antiseptics were the answer to stopping infection because they could kill germs. However, no one had ever used the chemicals on human wounds before. It was simply unheard of. What Lister needed was some kind of antiseptic that was caustic enough to kill

"In using the expression 'dressed antiseptically,' I do not mean merely 'dressed with an antiseptic,' but 'dressed so as to ensure absence of putrefaction.'"
—JOSEPH LISTER

Carbolic acid in test tubes undergoes various chemical reactions. Lister used carbolic acid as the first antiseptic.

germs without causing harm to a patient. He wrote, "Just as we may destroy lice on the head of a child . . . by poisonous applications which will not injure the scalp, so, I believe, we can use poisons on wounds to destroy bacteria without injuring the soft tissues of the patient."[9]

Then he read a report about the nearby city of Carlisle, and he was fascinated. The air in Carlisle was polluted by putrid-smelling odors from the garbage dump. The village pastures had also been a problem; sewage had been used as fertilizer and it had made the cattle very sick. Health and sanitation authorities used carbolic acid to treat the garbage and the pastures, and it had worked. The foul-smelling air was gone, and there was a marked reduction in disease among the cattle.

After reading the report, Lister began to consider the possibilities. Serious infections had foul-smelling odors that were caused by the decomposition of tissue. If carbolic acid could stop the stench of rotting garbage, he thought, the chemical may have killed the source of the odor: germs. So, he reasoned, the same principle should apply when human wounds were treated with it. If a wound were soaked in an antiseptic such as carbolic acid, it would undoubtedly stop bacteria from growing and multiplying. Lister decided that the only way to test such a treatment would be to use it on an actual patient. He obtained some of the thick, tarry substance. Because the antiseptic was experimental (and therefore risky), Lister would only use it on someone who had little or no chance of survival.

From Disappointment to Elation

In March 1865 Lister's first opportunity presented itself. A man who had been in a serious accident was brought to the Royal Infirmary with a badly crushed leg. He had waited many hours before seeking medical attention, so his condition was critical. By the time Lister saw him, his wound was badly infected and covered with pus, which was a sign of gangrene. Still, Lister believed he might be able to save the man. He cleaned the wound with carbolic acid, and then applied cloths that had been soaked in the chemical. Once the man's wound had begun to heal and he was physically stronger, Lister would be able to repair the broken bones in his leg.

The patient did not survive, however. His wound was so badly infected that nothing could possibly have saved him. Lister was deeply saddened by his death, but he knew he could not work miracles on someone who was so gravely ill. He vowed to try the treatment again—and next time, it would work.

When Lister treated Jimmy Greenlees in August 1865, it renewed his faith in the power of antiseptic treatment. The carbolic acid prevented the boy's wound from becoming infected, and it saved his life. Finally, Lister knew he had found the answer to killing bacteria and preventing infection: antiseptics.

The Germ Killer

After Jimmy's recovery, carbolic acid treatment became a standard practice in Lister's surgical wards. He used it to clean and disinfect wounds, and as a dressing to protect wounds from bacteria in the air. Surgical instruments were sterilized with the antiseptic, and Lister and his assistants used it to wipe their hands during surgery or while attending to patients.

Lister continued to treat one patient after another with carbolic acid, and the results were amazing. During a nine-month period, there were no further cases of gangrene or any other type of infection on Lister's wards, and the number of deaths declined sharply. The only disadvantage was that in its purest

Lister used carbolic acid to clean and disinfect everything in his surgical wards, including his own hands.

form, carbolic acid was a caustic substance that irritated skin. So Lister experimented by adding linseed oil and other ingredients that did not lessen the crucial antiseptic properties, but made the substance safer for delicate tissue.

Telling the World

Lister had often spoken to his students and fellow surgeons about his carbolic acid treatment. He had also discussed it extensively with his father-in-law. Now, Syme encouraged him to announce his findings to the world. Lister wrote a series of papers about his use of antiseptics. He discussed his germ theory, including how he had been inspired by the discoveries of Louis Pasteur. He included case histories of patients he had treated with carbolic acid, and described the sharp decline of infection and deaths in his wards. From March through July 1867, Lister's articles appeared in the highly respected medical journal *The Lancet*.

The articles piqued the interest of the medical world. In August, Lister was asked to make a presentation at a British Medical Association meeting in Dublin, Ireland. Speaking to an audience of the most prominent doctors and surgeons from all of Great Britain, he described his success with antiseptics. Some of the men in attendance were receptive to what Lister had to say, but most were highly skeptical. A few even spoke out against Louis Pasteur, declaring the whole germ theory to be nonsense. Nuland explains why medical professionals were so ready to doubt Lister's claims about germs and antiseptics:

> It was a great deal easier not to believe in them. Imagine a fifty-year-old surgeon at the height of his career. . . . One day, he attends a lecture delivered by a professor . . . during which he is told that little invisible creatures are his real enemy. . . . And finally, imagine the worst thing of all. Imagine what it must have felt like for such a surgeon to accept a theory that confronts him with the intolerable fact that for the previous fifteen years of his career he has been killing his patients by allowing into their wounds microbes which he should have been destroying.[10]

Scottish physician James Simpson condemned Lister's theories about germs and infection.

By far, Lister's most outspoken critic was James Simpson, a highly respected doctor who had invented chloroform anesthesia. Like Lister, Simpson had long been concerned with the high rate of infection and death in hospitals. In an article called "Hospitalism" he had quoted a number of bleak statistics and warned, "The man laid on the operating table in one of our surgical hospitals is exposed to more chances of death than the English soldier on the field of Waterloo."[11] However, as concerned as Simpson was about infection, he vehemently disagreed with Lister's answer to stopping it. He refused to believe that germs were the cause of infection, and he was against the use of antiseptics. Following the meeting in Dublin, Simpson wrote a series of letters to *The Lancet* in which he publicly denounced Lister and his findings.

Impressive Numbers

Lister was confused about why medical professionals were so ready to oppose his work with antiseptics—work that had proven to save lives. Especially perplexing was Simpson's antagonism toward him. He knew there had been deep-seated hostility between Simpson and Syme for many years, but he had not experienced it for himself until now. Even so, he refused to dwell on it. He felt that he should address Simpson's accusations, so he wrote several letters to *The Lancet*. True to his nature, though, he kept his responses informative and dignified, rather than matching Simpson's antagonistic tone.

In a later article for *The Lancet*, Lister reported some impressive statistics. Before antiseptics were used in his surgical wards, sixteen of every thirty-five people who were admitted had died. Once Lister began using his carbolic acid treatment, the number of deaths dropped to six out of forty patients—which was more than a 30 percent reduction. In addition, these numbers did not even account for the many patients who were able to avoid amputation because their wounds had healed so well. Lister wrote: "If the history of all the contused wounds of the hands and feet that have been treated in my wards during the last three years were recorded, including many compound fractures . . . it would be enough to convince the most [skeptical] of the advantages of the antiseptic system."[12]

Using antiseptics and sterilized surgical instruments, Lister saw a dramatic reduction in the death rate among his patients.

Better Ligatures

As Lister continued to see positive results from the use of carbolic acid, he began to consider other uses for antiseptics. One thing that had concerned him for years involved surgery on internal organs. In order to repair a major artery or blood vessel, the surgeon had to make a deep incision and tie the artery with a silk cord known as a ligature. Then he stitched the patient's skin back together, leaving the ends of the ligature outside the wound. Once the surgeon believed that blood had clotted over the artery, he pulled out the cord. The removal was necessary because bacteria could travel up the ligature and cause infection if it reached the internal wound. However, removing the ligature was difficult as well as dangerous. Many patients bled to death because the clot broke open when the cord was taken out. Lister was convinced that there had to be a better, safer way to perform this type of surgery.

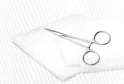

"Mr. Lister has done an important and lasting service to the cause of humanity and surgery by his unwearied attempts to eradicate septic diseases from surgical practice, and to make operations effectual and safe."
—EXCERPT FROM AN 1879 ARTICLE IN *THE LANCET*

At first he considered using carbolic acid to sterilize silk cord, which he believed would prevent infection from developing. If that were the case, perhaps the ligature would not have to be removed at all. It could be cut short at the time of surgery, and left inside the patient's body. He discovered, though, that silk had tiny fragments that were sharp enough to irritate delicate tissue. Then he came up with a better idea: catgut, a substance that was made from the intestines of sheep or other animals. Catgut was soft and supple, and was used to make strings

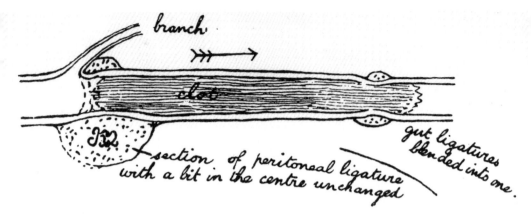

In this drawing from 1867, Lister details how he used catgut as a ligature on the carotid artery of a calf.

for musical instruments. Lister believed it would be perfect for ligatures. If it were properly sterilized, it would be able to stay inside a patient's body, where it would be naturally absorbed.

Successful Experiment

Lister obtained some catgut and experimented with it by operating on the carotid artery of a calf. First he soaked the ligature for four hours in a carbolic acid solution, and then he performed the surgery. His nephew, Rickman John Godlee, assisted him and later wrote about the experience: "I have a vivid recollection of the operation . . . the shaving and purification of the part, the meticulous attention to every antiseptic detail, the dressing formed of a towel soaked in carbolized oil; and my grandfather's alabaster Buddha on the mantelpiece contemplating with inscrutable gaze the services of beasts to men."[13] One month after the operation, the calf was still healthy. As a sacrifice on behalf of antiseptic research, the animal was slaughtered and select portions of it were sent to Lister for examination. After dissecting the tissue, Lister could see that his suspicions had been correct: The catgut had almost completely disappeared, and new tissue had grown in its place. Much to his delight, there was no sign of infection whatsoever.

To let medical professionals know about his discovery, Lister wrote an article entitled "Observations on Ligature of Arteries on the Antiseptic System." The article appeared in the *Lancet* in April 1869, and, as Lister expected, there were mixed reactions from surgeons. Some wrote that they had tried his catgut ligatures and were pleased with the result, while others had not fared so well. For years afterward, Lister continued experimenting with ligatures in order to improve them.

Life Changes

The same month that Lister's article about ligatures was published in *The Lancet*, he and Agnes received some disturbing news: Syme had suffered a severe stroke and was partially paralyzed. They traveled to Edinburgh to be with him, and were relieved to find that the paralysis was temporary. Over the next few months he recovered from the stroke, but his health had suffered. He knew he could not keep working and would have to retire. That meant a replacement would be needed for his position as the chair of clinical surgery at Edinburgh University, and there was only one person whom he wanted to take his place: Joseph Lister.

Lister applied for the position immediately. He was not sure that the university directors would want him, though. Edinburgh was Simpson's hometown, and the man had a great deal of influence with other medical professionals. However, on August 18, 1869, Lister received a letter confirming that he had been chosen for the job. In October, he and Agnes moved to back to Edinburgh.

Within a week of the move, a letter arrived from Upton House saying that Joseph Jackson Lister was gravely ill. Lister left immediately for England, where he spent five days with his father before he died. It was a sad and difficult time for Lister, and the loss of his father was extremely painful. He and Agnes returned to Upton one last time for the sale of the family home. Later, in a letter to his brother-in-law, Lister wrote, "I look back with a curious mingled feeling upon my last stay, as I suppose it was, in the old house where I was born, and . . . the predominant feeling is one of great sadness."[14]

A New Beginning

Not long after his father's death, Lister delivered his introductory address at Edinburgh University. He began by warmly praising Syme, who had long been his teacher, his mentor, and his friend: "We may all rejoice that our master is still among us, to cheer us by his presence and aid us by his counsel; and it is a source of great satisfaction to myself that, as I have the privilege of free access to his inexhaustible store of wisdom and experience, he will, in some sense, through me be still your teacher."[15]

A team of surgeons uses carbolic acid as a disinfectant during a procedure in this photo from the 1870s.

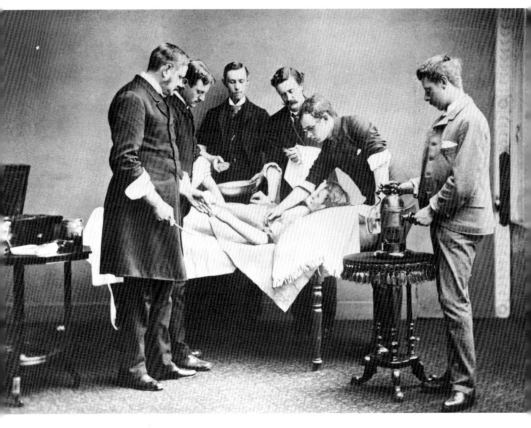

From the beginning, Lister was the university's most popular professor. His lectures were crowded with students who were eager to learn from the surgeon who had become so well known throughout Europe. Lister, too, was happy because he enjoyed teaching so much. He was able to use Syme's method of "clinical lectures," a practice that was frowned on in Glasgow. These lectures involved hands-on teaching while the students observed from tiered benches. A patient was wheeled into the lecture hall and placed on a table. Lister would explain the patient's affliction to the students, and then tell them what operation was necessary and why. Sometimes he even performed surgery in front of them so he could demonstrate how antiseptics were used during operations.

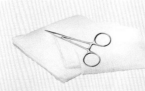

"His manner with strangers and young people had something of old-fashioned dignity handed down to him from the days when youth and age were separated by barriers that have now been swept away."

—SIR RICKMAN JOHN GODLEE, WRITING ABOUT HIS UNCLE, JOSEPH LISTER

Outside the university, Lister was quickly becoming known as one of Scotland's best surgeons. In addition to his work at the Royal Infirmary, his private practice was flourishing more than at any other time of his career. Also, even though his antiseptic treatment was still regarded as controversial, more and more surgeons reported positive results using it. During 1869 and 1870 *The Lancet* published a large number of letters and articles on Listerism. Most were favorable, although Lister still had many outspoken critics.

Simpson and Syme

One of the most critical was Simpson, who continued to speak out against Lister's antiseptic practices. He wrote and published a series of articles in support of his own solution for rampant infections, which was to burn down the hospitals. Simpson was known as an aggressive fighter. Because he suffered from a heart disease known as angina pectoris, his doctors often advised him not to overexert himself physically and emotionally. He would not listen, however, and in May 1870 Simpson died at the age of sixty.

Less than a month before Simpson's death, another of Edinburgh's most notable surgeons was taken ill. Syme suffered a second stroke, followed by a third stroke in May that was debilitating. He lost the ability to speak or swallow, and had to be fed through a tube. Agnes lovingly cared for her father as his health continued to decline, and he died on June 26, 1870. Syme was buried four days later, and an obituary written by Lister paid a proper tribute to him: "The hostility which he excited in a few was greatly outweighed by the friendship he inspired in the many. Rarely is it granted to any one to attach to himself the enduring love and admiration of so large a number of his fellow-men. . . . Mr. Syme, perfect gentleman, and a good, as well as a great man."[16]

Losing Syme was difficult for Lister. The two men had been colleagues and friends for many years, and he had felt nearly as close to Syme as he had his own father. Lister had long been encouraged and inspired by Syme, and he would deeply miss him. He would never forget the ongoing support and loyalty that Syme had shown through his work with antiseptic surgery.

War Casualties

Soon after Syme's death, a war broke out between France and a European kingdom known as Prussia (present-day Germany). It was known as the Franco-Prussian War, and it only lasted a year—but in that short time, tens of thousands of soldiers were killed and thousands more were severely wounded. The men were carried, injured and bleeding, into overcrowded hospitals where nearly all of them died from gangrene and other infections. Lister could imagine the horrors of the battlefield, and he wanted to help. He sent bottles of carbolic acid to field stations, but they were returned to him unopened. He later learned that

This illustration depicts the siege of Paris in the Franco-Prussian War, during which thousands of soldiers died of infected wounds.

the German and French surgeons either did not know what to do with the antiseptic or did not want to bother using it.

Lister was frustrated. He knew if doctors and surgeons would use carbolic acid, it would cut down on infection in military hospitals, just as it had in civilian hospitals. He wrote a four-page pamphlet entitled "A Method of Antiseptic Treatment Applicable to Wounded Soldiers in the Present War." In the booklet, Lister described how wounds should be treated with carbolic acid, both on the battlefield and in hospitals. He also emphasized the importance of using the antiseptic to clean surgical instruments, as well as to cleanse surgeons' hands between operations. In September 1870 the pamphlet was published in the *British Medical Journal*.

"Triumphal March"

After the war, German and French surgeons traveled to Edinburgh to meet with Lister. They had seen many thousands of cases of gangrene and other infections, as well as amputations that almost always led to death. If antiseptics could prevent such tragedy in the future, they wanted to learn about them.

During the following years, surgeons throughout Europe began to speak out in support of Lister. One of his most avid supporters was a German surgeon named Ritter von Nussbaum, who practiced at Munich Hospital, one of the unhealthiest hospitals in Germany. As many as 80 percent of the patients admitted there with serious wounds contracted gangrene. Desperate to put a stop to the rampant infection, von Nussbaum adopted Lister's antiseptic practices—and the results were astounding. Von Nussbaum described them at a meeting of the German

A church is used as a military hospital during the Franco-Prussian War. Military doctors did not use Lister's carbolic acid to treat wounded soldiers.

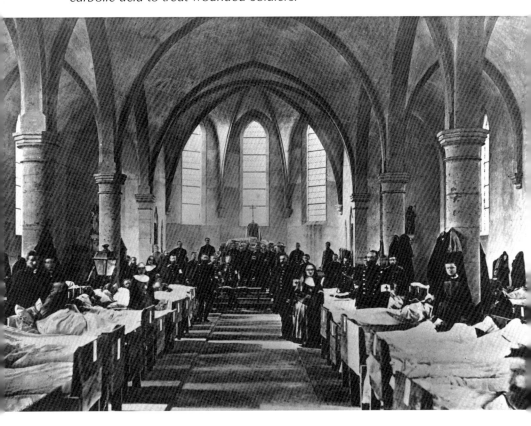

Lister, top right, is shown with other doctors at King's College in London. In 1877 Lister was named head of surgery at the college.

Surgical Congress in 1875: "Look at my sick wards recently ravaged by death. I can only say that my assistants and my nurses and I are overwhelmed with joy. It is with the greatest zeal that we undergo all the extra pains required by the treatment."[17] Von Nussbaum also wrote a short book on antiseptic treatment that was later translated into French, Italian, and Greek. As the book's circulation grew, so did European acceptance of antiseptics.

In the summer of 1875 Lister and his wife left for an extended European trip. They traveled to France and Italy, and then went to Germany, where they visited hospitals in Munich, Berlin, and several other major cities. Along the way, they met with professors and surgeons who told of their success with antiseptic treatment. They also visited clinics and hospitals to train people how to properly use antiseptics. An issue of *The Lancet* that was published in June of 1875 described Lister's German visit as a "triumphal march." After years of being doubted for his belief in antiseptics, Lister was finally getting the recognition and respect he had long deserved.

Leaving Scotland

Yet even though Lister was being hailed by surgeons throughout Europe, there was one major city where his antiseptic practices were still not accepted: London. A few younger surgeons had started to adopt Lister's antiseptic practices.

However, most of London's older, well-established doctors and surgeons were still resistant to his theories about germs—and these men made it clear that they wanted nothing whatsoever to do with antiseptics.

London was the center of the United Kingdom and a city with many influential medical professionals. In order for antiseptics to be universally accepted, Lister knew he would have to win the approval of London surgeons. He also knew that this would not be possible if he remained in Scotland. Even though he had been born and raised in England, he had lived away for so long that he was now considered a foreigner. Unless he practiced medicine in a London hospital, people in England would never pay attention to what he had to say.

By this time, Lister was fifty years old. He and Agnes loved Edinburgh and had spent some of their happiest years there. He was revered by his students and highly regarded by his fellow surgeons, and he thoroughly enjoyed his work. Still, when he was offered a position as chair of surgery at the medical school of King's College in London, he decided to accept. It was a difficult decision, and many times he doubted himself for making it. In his biography of his uncle, Godlee explains why Lister felt it was the only choice he could make:

> Lister was now a man with a mission. The antiseptic doctrine had been accepted in every part of the world that counted, except London. . . . The importance of converting the greatest centre of learning and education in England justified almost any sacrifice, and it seemed as if the only way of convincing Londoners were to let them see how he actually carried out the treatment himself, and the results he was able to obtain.[18]

An Uncomfortable Start

On September 11, 1877, Lister and his wife moved to London. Three weeks later he gave his introductory lecture at King's College, which he called "On the Nature of Fermentation." His intention was to convince people that he was right about bacteria and antiseptics. The lecture theater was filled with scientists, surgeons, and students, all of whom were curious about this person they considered a bit strange. Lister started by showing drawings and diagrams of germs. Then he showed test tubes and beakers that contained milk and other fluids in various stages of fermentation, and he discussed the experiments he had performed.

The audience's reception was nothing like those Lister had experienced in Edinburgh. Whereas his previous lectures had been met with eagerness and enthusiasm, he now gazed out at a sea of confused expressions. The surgeons were respectful, but they did not seem to understand the points Lister was making. Watson Cheyne, a surgeon who traveled to London to be one of Lister's assistants, describes the reaction:

> Perhaps not unnaturally they expected to be told about the revolution in surgery which Lister had inaugurated, and instead they had to sit for an hour listening to details of a series of experiments which proved that . . . fermentation of milk was due to a particular bacterium! The expression on the faces of the audience was very interesting and rather amusing; the majority of the surgeons present could not understand what the lactic fermentation of milk had to do with surgery.[19]

What Lister found most disturbing was the reaction of the students. He had always gotten along so well with young people, and his students in Edinburgh were fiercely loyal to him. These students, however, were disrespectful, and some even heckled him. They scuffed their feet loudly on the floor, and when he talked about milk, they made mooing sounds. Lister did his best to ignore them so he could finish his speech.

His subsequent lectures were equally disappointing. Few students bothered to attend, and those who did typically straggled in long after the lecture had begun. Again, this was in stark contrast to Edinburgh, where hundreds of students were eager to hear whatever Lister had to say. In London he felt fortunate if twenty students showed up. It was obvious that aspiring surgeons in England did not care to learn about antiseptics.

The Turning Point

At the hospital, Lister found things uncomfortable as well. He immediately clashed with the nursing staff, who were set in their ways. Lister's insistence on cleanliness and antiseptics was far from well received. He also started out badly with the other surgeons. Before leaving Edinburgh, Lister had criticized the teaching methods used in London because they did not involve clinical instruction. His remarks ended up in a newspaper, and the London surgeons were insulted. One of them, John Wood, was resentful of Lister for another reason of his own. He had worked at King's College for many years, and had expected to be appointed chair of surgery. To appease him, Lister agreed that the two would have equal status among the staff.

As time went by, the medical students and other surgeons began to accept and admire Lister. Once they got to know him, they found that their preconceptions about him had been wrong, as Godlee explains: "Far from being the conceited and overbearing boaster they had pictured to themselves, he proved to be a humble-minded and courteous gentleman who treated them with respect and commanded the same in return."[20]

Lister's real test came when he saw a patient who was admitted with a fractured kneecap. The bones in his knee were badly smashed, but it was not a compound fracture because he had no open wound. If left alone, his knee would eventually heal on its own. However, Lister knew the man's leg would never be normal without surgery—yet the type of operation he had in mind was extremely risky. It involved converting a simple fracture into a compound fracture, which almost always resulted in infection and amputation.

Lister was confident in his ability to perform the surgery, as well as being able to avoid infection by using antiseptics. With the patient's consent, he went ahead with the operation. He cut the knee joint to expose the broken bones, and bound the bone fragments together with silver wire. The last step was to stitch the wound together and apply an antiseptic dressing.

The operation was a complete success. The patient did not develop infection or any other complications, and several months later his knee had healed. Once again, Lister had proven that antiseptics had the ability to prevent infection and save lives.

Good Years

Word quickly spread about the successful operation, and respect for Lister grew. Other surgeons saw the value of antiseptics and began using them on their own wards. Wood, who had often spoken out against their use, personally asked Lister to instruct him in antiseptic techniques. As a result, King's College Hospital saw a marked reduction in infection and deaths. Lister had finally achieved the goal he set for himself when he first went to King's College: London had embraced his antiseptic practices.

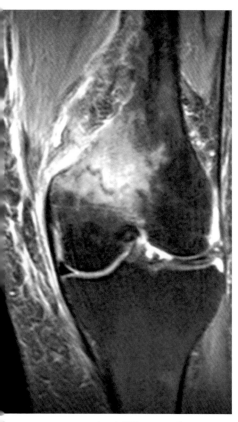

An MRI scan shows a knee with a fractured femur. Lister's risky operation on a patient with a fractured kneecap was unheard of in his day.

Along with increased admiration from his peers, Lister also received many honors in the following years. In 1880 he was given honorary doctorates from Cambridge and Oxford universities. In 1883 he was awarded France's coveted Boudet Prize for his application of Louis Pasteur's discoveries to medicine. That same year, England's Queen Victoria designated him a baronet, which was one step below the title of baron. Medical societies everywhere elected him as an honorary member of their organizations. His name had become famous throughout the world.

54

The Long-Awaited Meeting

Lister was pleased that he had gained so much respect, but he had never been interested in being famous. All he ever wanted was for people to understand that germs caused infection, and that antiseptics could destroy germs.

Throughout the years, he never forgot about the person who was responsible for helping him make that connection, and he hoped to someday meet him. In 1892 his wish was granted. He and Agnes were invited to attend a celebration in honor of Louis Pasteur's seventieth birthday, and Lister was asked to give a presentation.

The Listers traveled to Paris for the December 27 event, which was held at the Sorbonne, a noted university. The large theater was crowded to overflowing with more than 2,500 people. There were esteemed scientists from all over the world, as well as government and military officials, distinguished university professors, and hundreds of students.

Pasteur, who was in poor health, was ushered into the theater leaning heavily on the arm of the president of France. After speeches by several officials, it was Lister's turn to speak, and he spared no words in his praise of Pasteur. With emotion in his voice, he talked about the profound difference the great chemist had made, and how invaluable his discoveries were to medicine and surgery. When the presentation was over, Pasteur—as physically weak as he was—rose to his feet and embraced Lister, kissing him on both cheeks. Of all the triumphant moments Lister had experienced in his life, none meant more than being embraced by the great Louis Pasteur. Three months later, he received a telegram from Pasteur. It was notification that Lister had been awarded the highest scientific honor in France: election as an associate of the prestigious Académie des Sciences.

Heartbreak in Italy

Following the trip to Paris, Lister and his wife decided to take a vacation. They traveled to the Italian Riviera, where they stayed in a town called Rapallo. They had been there for about a week when Agnes developed a chill, and Lister summoned a local

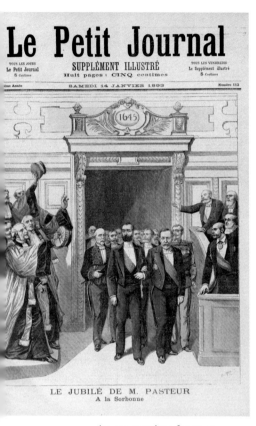

Le Petit Journal

TOUS LES JOURS
Le Petit Journal
5 Centimes

SUPPLÉMENT ILLUSTRÉ
Huit pages : CINQ centimes

TOUS LES VENDREDIS
Le Supplément illustré
5 Centimes

ème Année   SAMEDI 14 JANVIER 1893   Numéro 112

LE JUBILÉ DE M. PASTEUR
A la Sorbonne

An engraving from a Paris newspaper shows Pasteur's seventieth birthday celebration in 1892, where Lister and Pasteur finally met.

physician. As a surgeon, he was not qualified to treat her. His greatest fear was that she had pneumonia, and the physician confirmed that he was right. Over the next four days, Agnes grew progressively more ill and her condition rapidly deteriorated.

Lister would not leave his wife's bedside. They had been married for thirty-seven years, and she was not only his wife, but his trusted confidante, his research associate, and his best friend. Yet even though he had devoted his entire career to saving people's lives, he could not save her. On April 12, 1893, Agnes Lister died at the age of fifty-seven. Lister traveled back to London alone, accompanied by her coffin. She was buried in West Hamstead Cemetery.

A Bittersweet Time

After his wife's death, Lister found it difficult to go on. Cheyne later wrote that losing her "broke him down and changed entirely the current of his life."[21] His friends tried to comfort him, but it was not possible. A year before, he had reached the mandatory age for retirement from King's College and resigned his position there. He did agree to accept the post of foreign secretary for the Royal Society, and in 1894 he was elected president of the organization. When Pasteur died in 1895, Lister traveled to Paris to deliver a final tribute to the man he had revered for so many years.

In 1897 Lister received his most prestigious designation: Queen Victoria elevated his title to that of baron. He was the first medical professional ever to achieve such a title. Yet in spite of all the honors that continued to be showered upon him, he had lost the passion that fueled him for most of his life. Cheyne explains: "The great brain gradually became tired, his memory failed, and he began to long for the time to come when, as he hoped and firmly believed, he would meet his wife and his friends again and commence a new life."[22]

Through the following years, Lister continued to write articles that frequently appeared in *The Lancet* and the *British Medical Journal*. However, his health and sight were rapidly failing. On his eightieth birthday, in 1907, he was honored at a grand celebration in Vienna, Austria, known as the Lister Meeting. More than five hundred guests attended, and when Lister's portrait was projected above the platform, the audience gave him a standing ovation.

The World Loses a Hero

By 1909 Lister was almost completely blind and he could no longer read or write. Godlee describes this time as extremely sad for the family: "He looked wistfully at us and told us he had 'so much to say.' But alas, he was not able to give expression to these last thoughts."[23] Lister

Joseph Lister forever changed the world of medicine with his revolutionary work in understanding and preventing infection.

lived for three more years, although he was in very poor health, and on February 10, 1912, he died at the age of eighty-five.

Lister's funeral was held at the most famous cathedral in Europe, London's Westminster Abbey. People came from all over the world to pay their last respects to the man who had devoted his life to saving people from the scourge of infection. Because he was such a hero in the world of medicine, many people wanted him to be buried in the abbey's cemetery. However, Lister had left explicit instructions in his will that he was to be buried in the West Hamstead Cemetery, beside his beloved Agnes. On February 16, 1912, he was laid to rest there. A simple marker, which was indicative of his humility, simply listed his name, his date of birth, and his date of death.

The Father of Antiseptics

Joseph Lister did not invent a lifesaving drug or develop a revolutionary type of surgery. What he did was discover how antiseptics could prevent infection and save lives, and he devoted his entire career to teaching those principles to others. He was a humble man whose Quaker upbringing made him shy away from any sort of personal recognition or fame. All he cared about was helping people. Yet in spite of his quiet demeanor and simple ways, he was not afraid to stand up for what he believed in. Even though he was often scorned and ridiculed, and endured the hostility of surgeons who thought him a fool, it never stopped him from fighting for what he knew was right. For those reasons, Joseph Lister is one of medicine's greatest heroes.

IMPORTANT DATES

1827   Joseph Lister is born in the English village of Upton.

1844   Lister moves to London and attends University College.

1847   Lister graduates with a bachelor of arts degree; enrolls in University College's medical school.

1850   Lister begins surgical residency at University College Hospital.

1852   Lister graduates from University College with a bachelor of medicine degree (with honors).

1853   Lister travels to Scotland to meet well-known surgeon and professor James Syme; decides to remain there and accepts position as Syme's supernumerary clerk.

1855   Lister is elected a Fellow of Edinburgh's Royal College of Surgeons.

1856   Lister marries Agnes Syme, James Syme's eldest daughter.

1860   Lister accepts position as professor of surgery at the University of Glasgow; he and his wife move from Edinburgh to Glasgow.

1861   Lister is elected surgeon to the Glasgow Royal Infirmary.

1865   Lister learns about the research of Louis Pasteur; extensively studies Pasteur's writings and makes connection between fermentation of liquid and putrefaction of wounds; uses carbolic acid as disinfectant in surgery.

1868   Lister develops a new technique for surgery using catgut ligature.

1869   James Syme suffers a stroke, and retires from position of chair of clinical Surgery at Edinburgh University; Lister is hired to replace him; he and his wife move back to Edinburgh; his father, Joseph Jackson Lister dies.

1870   Syme suffers another debilitating stroke and dies; Franco-Prussian War breaks out; Lister writes pamphlet entitled "A Method of Antiseptic Treatment Applicable to Wounded Soldiers in the Present War."

1875   Joseph and Agnes Lister begin extensive trip throughout Europe.

1877   Lister accepts position as chair of surgery at the medical school of London's King's College; he and his wife move to London.

1880   Lister receives honorary doctorates from Cambridge and Oxford universities.

1883   Lister is awarded France's coveted Boudet Prize; Queen Victoria designates Lister a baronet.

1892   The Listers travel to France in honor of Louis Pasteur's seventieth birthday; Lister gives presentation and is publicly embraced by Pasteur.

1893   While on a vacation in Italy, Agnes Lister develops pneumonia and dies.

1895   Lister is elected president of the Royal Society; Louis Pasteur dies in Paris.

1897   Lister is designated baron by Queen Victoria.

1907   Celebration in Vienna, Austria, in honor of Lister's eightieth birthday.

1912   Lister dies at the age of eighty-five; after a funeral at London's famous Westminster Abbey cathedral, he is buried next to his wife in the West Hamstead Cemetery.

FOR MORE INFORMATION

BOOKS

John Bankston, *Joseph Lister and the Story of Antiseptics*. Hockessin, DE: Mitchell Lane, 2004.

Fiona MacDonald, *Louis Pasteur: Father of Modern Medicine*. Woodbridge, CT: Blackbirch Press: 2001.

Iris Noble, *The Courage of Dr. Lister*. New York: Julian Messner, 1960.

Robert Snedden, *Scientists and Discoveries*. Chicago: Heinemann Library, 2000.

PERIODICALS

Mick Foran, "Antiseptic Surgery: Medical Advance or Quack Fad?" *Old News* (July/August 2000): 8–9.

"Joseph Lister 1827–1912," *Monkeyshines on Great Inventors* (January 1997): 57.

John Hudson Tiner, "Deadly Doctors," *Nature Friend* (July 2003): 18–20.

———, "Doctor Lister Fights Infection," *Nature Friend* (August 2002): 18–20.

WEB SITES

History of Medicine www.abpischools.org.uk/resources04/history/index.asp. Maintained by the Association of the British Pharmaceutical Industry, this informative site traces the evolution of medicine throughout history. Includes some interesting facts about cleanliness, hygiene, surgery, and antiseptics in the nineteenth century.

History of Science www.farmors.gloucs.sch.uk/science/hist.htm. A good collection of information on noted scientists, including Joseph Lister and Louis Pasteur.

GLOSSARY

achromatic lens: A type of lens system that greatly improved the microscope.

anaerobic: The absence of oxygen.

antiseptic: A substance that can stop the growth of bacteria and prevent infection.

bacteria: Living microscopic organisms that can lead to infection or disease.

cadaver: The dead body of a human being.

carbolic acid: A chemical derived from coal tar that was originally used as an antiseptic.

gangrene: A disease that involves the rotting away of body tissue usually as a result of severe infection.

microbe: A microscopic organism, such as a germ.

putrefaction: Decomposition or decay.

sepsis: Infection of the blood or tissues.

suppuration: Festering or the formation of pus as a result of infection.

NOTES

1. Richard B. Fisher, *Joseph Lister: 1827–1912*. New York: Stein and Day, 1977, p. 28.
2. Quoted in Rickman John Godlee, *Lord Lister*. London: Macmillan, 1918, p. 13.
3. Rhoda Truax, *Joseph Lister: Father of Modern Surgery*. Indianapolis/New York: Bobbs-Merrill, 1944, p. 37.
4. Quoted in Fisher, *Joseph Lister*, p. 89.
5. Quoted in Godlee, *Lord Lister*, p. 91.
6. Sherwin B. Nuland, *Doctors: The Biography of Medicine*. New York: Knopf, 1988, p. 362.
7. Truax, *Joseph Lister*, pp. 91–92.
8. Quoted in Nuland, *Doctors*, p. 364.
9. Quoted in Nuland, *Doctors*, p. 364.
10. Nuland, *Doctors*, p. 370.
11. Quoted in Nuland, *Doctors*, p. 346.
12. Quoted in Nuland, *Doctors*, p. 366.
13. Godlee, *Lord Lister*, p. 231.
14. Quoted in Godlee, *Lord Lister*, p. 244.
15. Quoted in Fisher, *Joseph Lister*, p. 171.
16. Quoted in Godlee, *Lord Lister*, p. 253.
17. Quoted in Nuland, *Doctors*, p. 373.
18. Godlee, *Lord Lister*, p. 402.
19. William Watson Cheyne, *Lister and His Achievement*. London: Longmans, Green, 1925, p. 33.
20. Godlee, *Lord Lister*, p. 422.
21. Cheyne, *Lister and His Achievement*, p. 37.
22. Cheyne, *Lister and His Achievement*, p. 38.
23. Godlee, *Lord Lister*, p. 592.

INDEX